QUICK & EASY MEALS
FOR BUSY MOMS
120 TASTY RECIPES

BARBOUR
PUBLISHING

Inspiration at your fingertips!

Looking for a simple way to bring new life to your kitchen? This book is for you. Within these pages, you'll find dozens of tasty recipes that are easy to prepare and are a delight to share with family and friends.

Finding a recipe is as easy as flipping through the book. At the bottom of each page, you'll see a color that corresponds to one of five categories:

BUSY MORNING BREAKFASTS

ON-THE-GO LUNCHES

ONE-DISH DINNERS

FAST AND FESTIVE MEALS

DESSERTS AND SNACKS

So set up this little book on your countertop, flip page after page for new culinary inspiration and kitchen tips and tricks, and you might just find a little encouragement for your soul in the process. Enjoy!

BUSY MORNING BREAKFASTS

Great is his faithfulness; his mercies begin afresh each morning.
LAMENTATIONS 3:23

SAUSAGE CASSEROLE

4 cups cubed bread
2 cups shredded sharp cheddar cheese
2 (12 ounce) cans evaporated milk
10 large eggs, lightly beaten
½ teaspoon dry mustard
¼ teaspoon onion powder
¼ teaspoon black pepper
½ teaspoon salt
12 ounces breakfast sausage, cooked and drained

Place bread in greased 9x13-inch baking dish. Sprinkle with cheese.
Combine remaining ingredients except sausage. Pour evenly over bread
and cheese. Sprinkle with sausage. Cover with foil and refrigerate
overnight. Bake, covered, for 1 hour at 325 degrees.

EASY BRUNCH CASSEROLE

2 cups stuffing mix
2 cups milk
½ pound maple sausage, cooked and crumbled
6 eggs
1 cup shredded cheddar cheese
½ teaspoon salt
¼ teaspoon pepper

Mix all ingredients in large bowl. Spoon into greased 9x13-inch baking pan. Bake at 350 degrees for 45 minutes or until knife inserted in center comes out clean.

HANDY CONVERSIONS

1 teaspoon = 5 milliliters
1 tablespoon = 15 milliliters
1 fluid ounce = 30 milliliters
1 cup = 250 milliliters
1 pint = 2 cups (or 16 fluid ounces)
1 quart = 4 cups (or 2 pints or 32 fluid ounces)
1 gallon = 16 cups (or 4 quarts)
1 peck = 8 quarts
1 bushel = 4 pecks
1 pound = 454 grams

Fahrenheit	Celsius
250°–300°	121°–149°
300°–325°	149°–163°
325°–350°	163°–177°
375°	191°
400°–425°	204°–218°

HAM 'N' CHEESE PIE

1½ cups cubed fully cooked ham
1 cup shredded cheddar cheese
¼ cup sweet onion, chopped
½ cup baking mix
1 cup milk
¼ teaspoon salt
⅛ teaspoon pepper
2 eggs
Tomatoes, sliced (optional)

Sprinkle ham, cheese, and onion in greased 9-inch pie plate. Mix remaining ingredients except tomatoes and pour into pie plate. Bake for 35 minutes at 400 degrees or until knife inserted in center comes out clean. Cool 5 minutes. Garnish with sliced tomatoes if desired.

FRENCH TOAST CASSEROLE

1 loaf cinnamon raisin bread, cubed
6 large eggs, beaten
3 cups milk
2 teaspoons vanilla extract
Powdered sugar
Syrup

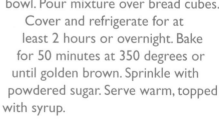

Layer bread cubes evenly in a greased 9x13-inch baking dish. Beat eggs, milk, and vanilla in a separate bowl. Pour mixture over bread cubes. Cover and refrigerate for at least 2 hours or overnight. Bake for 50 minutes at 350 degrees or until golden brown. Sprinkle with powdered sugar. Serve warm, topped with syrup.

BLUEBERRY BANANA MUFFINS

2 ripe bananas
½ cup milk
1 large egg, slightly beaten
2 tablespoons vegetable oil
2 teaspoons fresh lemon juice
1 cup white flour
½ cup wheat flour
½ cup sugar
¼ cup quick oats
2 teaspoons baking powder
½ teaspoon salt
1½ cups blueberries

Mix together the bananas, milk, egg, oil, and lemon juice. Add flours, sugar, oats, baking powder, and salt and mix until just moistened. Lightly fold in blueberries. Fill each prepared muffin cup ¾ full. Bake for 20 minutes at 400 degrees or until golden brown.

SAUSAGE OMELET

6 eggs
Butter
4 sausage links, precooked and sliced
½ cup cheddar cheese
Salt and pepper to taste

Beat eggs until well combined. Place in buttered skillet and scramble. Add sausage and cheese. Cook for 3 to 5 more minutes until sausage is heated through. Salt and pepper to taste.

MEXICAN EGGS

2 tablespoons butter
½ cup chopped tomato
¼ cup finely chopped onion
1 (4 ounce) can diced green chilies
½ cup crushed corn tortilla chips
4 eggs, beaten until frothy
Salt to taste
½ cup shredded cheddar cheese

Heat butter in skillet and sauté chopped tomato, onion, and green chilies for 1 minute. Add tortilla chips. Pour eggs into the skillet over other ingredients and cook, stirring often, until mixture sets. Sprinkle with salt and cheese.

BANANA MILKSHAKE SMOOTHIE

1 cup crushed ice
2 large bananas
1 (15 ounce) can pineapple chunks, undrained
1 cup skim milk
1 cup banana yogurt

Place ice in blender. Add remaining ingredients. Puree until smooth.
Serve immediately.

BACON PIE

12 slices bacon, crisply cooked and crumbled
3 slices baby swiss cheese
⅓ cup chopped onion
½ cup baking mix
1 cup milk
⅛ teaspoon pepper
2 eggs

Sprinkle bacon, cheese, and onions in greased 9-inch pie plate. Stir remaining ingredients until blended. Pour into pie plate. Bake for 35 minutes at 400 degrees or until knife inserted in center comes out clean. Cool 5 minutes before serving.

MESSY EGG CLEANUP

Egg-based foods can be hard to clean off plates and utensils.
Sprinkle the dishes with some salt right after the meal.
The salt reacts with the egg and makes for easier cleanup.

BANANA OAT MUFFINS

¾ cup buttermilk
3 ripe bananas
1 large egg, lightly beaten
2 tablespoons vegetable oil
1 teaspoon grated orange peel
⅓ cup brown sugar
1½ cups quick oats
1 cup flour
1 teaspoon baking powder
½ teaspoon baking soda
¼ teaspoon ground cinnamon
¼ teaspoon salt

Combine buttermilk, bananas, egg, oil, and orange peel. Mix well. Add remaining ingredients and mix until just moistened. Fill each prepared muffin cup ¾ full. Bake for 20 minutes at 400 degrees or until golden brown.

PEACH SMOOTHIE

1 cup crushed ice
2 cups fresh or frozen peaches, peeled and sliced
½ cup pineapple juice
½ cup milk
¼ cup vanilla yogurt

Place ice in bottom of blender. Add remaining ingredients. Puree until smooth. Serve immediately.

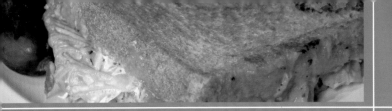

ON-THE-GO
LUNCHES

*"Yes, I am the vine; you are the branches.
Those who remain in me, and I in them, will produce much fruit.
For apart from me you can do nothing."*
JOHN 15:5

TUNA MELTS

1 (5 ounce) can flaked tuna, drained
1 hard-boiled egg, peeled and chopped
2 onions, chopped
1 tablespoon sweet relish
1 cup shredded cheddar cheese
¼ cup mayonnaise
1 teaspoon dijon mustard
4 buns, split

Mix together all ingredients except buns. Spoon tuna mixture into split buns. Wrap each bun tightly in foil. Place in oven and bake for 15 minutes at 400 degrees. Serve warm.

BROILED PEANUT BUTTER SANDWICHES

English muffins
1 teaspoon butter per sandwich
1 tablespoon peanut butter per sandwich
1 teaspoon honey per sandwich
Raisins

Spread English muffin with butter, peanut butter, and honey. Top with a few raisins. Wrap in foil and broil on low until warm.

Tired of preparing the same dishes all the time?
Make it a priority to try a new recipe each week.
Not only will you expand your culinary skills,
but chances are there's a new family favorite
waiting to make an appearance on your table.

DELI STROMBOLI

1 tube refrigerated pizza crust
1 tablespoon dijon mustard
1 tablespoon mayonnaise
¼ pound deli corned beef
¼ pound deli turkey breast
¼ pound sliced swiss cheese

On a cookie sheet, unfold pizza crust and flatten into a large rectangle. Spread mustard and mayonnaise over crust. Layer deli meats and cheese evenly over the crust. Roll up and pinch the seams. Cut a slit in the top for steam to escape. Bake for 15 to 18 minutes at 400 degrees or until golden brown.

4 slices deli ham
4 slices white bread
4 slices American cheese

Put 1 slice of ham on each slice of bread. Top with cheese. Put on a cookie sheet and bake at 350 degrees for 5 minutes or until cheese bubbles.

BROCCOLI LUNCH SALAD

1 cup mayonnaise
2 tablespoons cider vinegar
2 tablespoons sugar
2 bunches raw broccoli, chopped
1 cup sunflower seeds
½ cup raisins
6 slices cooked bacon, crumbled
½ cup cooked chicken breast, chopped

Mix together mayonnaise, vinegar, and sugar. Blend well. Put chopped broccoli in large bowl. Add mixture and remaining ingredients. Mix well.

PEPPERONI ROLL-UPS

4 to 6 slices of turkey pepperoni per roll-up
1 flour tortilla per roll-up
1 slice of provolone cheese per roll-up
Marinara sauce for dipping (optional)

Place pepperoni on soft tortilla. Top with cheese and roll up. Heat in microwave for 45 seconds or until cheese is melted. Dip in marinara sauce, if desired.

TURKEY QUESADILLAS

4 flour tortillas
4 teaspoons butter
4 teaspoons dijon mustard
8 slices deli turkey breast
2 cups shredded Monterey Jack cheese

Spread one side of each tortilla with butter. Flip the tortillas over and spread one teaspoon of mustard. Cover mustard with two turkey breast slices and ½ cup of cheese. Fold in half. Place quesadillas, buttered side down in a non-stick skillet. Cook 1 to 2 minutes on each side until golden brown.

ENGLISH MUFFIN PIZZA

1 English muffin
3 tablespoons spaghetti sauce
4 slices pepperoni
¼ cup shredded mozzarella cheese
Dash oregano

Split English muffin and place the two halves on baking sheet. Top each muffin half with half of the sauce, half of the pepperoni, and half of the cheese. Sprinkle with a dash of oregano. Bake for 4 to 6 minutes at 350 degrees until cheese is golden brown and bubbly.

When cutting up a whole head of lettuce,
always use this nifty tip:
To get the core out,
just give the head's core a whack on the countertop.
Then give the core a twist, and it comes right out.

GRILLED BACON AND CHEESE

1½ teaspoons butter
4 slices wheat bread
8 slices cheddar cheese
4 slices precooked bacon

Spread ¾ teaspoon butter on one side of each slice of bread. Fill each sandwich with cheese and bacon. Cook in a skillet for 1 to 3 minutes on first side, then flip and cook another 1 to 3 minutes until light brown.

GRILLED TOMATO AND CHEESE SANDWICHES

3 teaspoons butter
4 slices sourdough bread
2 slices cheddar cheese
1 tomato, thinly sliced

Spread ¾ teaspoon butter on one side of each slice of bread. Fill each sandwich with 1 slice of cheese and half the tomato. Cook in a skillet for 1 to 3 minutes on first side, then flip and cook another 1 to 3 minutes until light brown.

ROAST BEEF WRAP

2 teaspoons cream cheese
1 large flour tortilla
3 to 4 thin slices roast beef
1 lettuce leaf
1 tomato slice

Spread cream cheese on the tortilla. Add roast beef and warm for 10 to 15 seconds in microwave. Add lettuce and tomato and roll up.

ONE-DISH
DINNERS

*Then the earth will yield its harvests,
and God, our God, will richly bless us.*
PSALM 67:6

BBQ CHICKEN FAJITAS

1½ cups instant white rice, uncooked
1½ cups hot water
1 tablespoon taco seasoning mix
4 small boneless, skinless chicken breasts
4 tablespoons prepared barbecue sauce
1 green bell pepper, cut into strips
1 red bell pepper, cut into strips
½ cup chunky salsa
½ cup Mexican-style finely shredded cheese
Tortillas

Preheat oven to 400 degrees. Combine rice, water, and taco seasoning and spoon onto greased heavy-duty foil or foil packet. Top with remaining ingredients except tortillas, spreading barbecue sauce on top of chicken. Seal foil well, into a pouch, allowing room for the heat to circulate. Bake for 35 minutes or until chicken is no longer pink in the center. Let stand for 5 minutes before serving. Serve with warm tortillas.

PARMESAN CHICKEN DINNER

2 cloves garlic, minced
¼ cup Italian dressing
4 small boneless, skinless chicken breasts
¼ teaspoon black pepper
1 teaspoon basil, divided
1 (10 ounce) package frozen mixed vegetables, thawed
1 teaspoon salt
2 tablespoons grated Parmesan cheese
Pasta (optional)

Sauté garlic and dressing together in a large skillet over medium heat for 1 minute. Add chicken and season with black pepper and ¾ teaspoon basil. Cook 5 minutes on each side or until chicken is no longer pink. Add vegetables to skillet and sprinkle with remaining basil and salt. Cook for 3 more minutes, stirring occasionally. Top with cheese. Serve alone or with pasta.

Make a habit of thanking the Lord before each meal. After all, He's the one who's given us such abundance; because of His goodness, we can eat our fill and not go hungry. Take turns giving thanks around the dinner table. Have each family member participate. Prepare to be amazed at how the Lord has blessed each one of you.

FETA CHICKEN AND RICE

4 to 5 boneless, skinless chicken breasts
2 tablespoons lemon juice, divided
½ teaspoon salt
¼ teaspoon pepper
1 (4 ounce) package crumbled feta cheese
¼ cup diced fresh tomatoes
¼ cup green bell pepper, chopped fine
¼ cup fresh parsley, chopped
Rice

Arrange chicken in 9x13-inch baking dish. Sprinkle with 1 tablespoon lemon juice. Season with salt and pepper. Top with feta cheese and sprinkle remaining lemon juice on top. Bake for 35 to 40 minutes at 350 degrees or until chicken is cooked through. Sprinkle with tomatoes, bell pepper, and parsley. Serve hot over rice.

LEMON CHICKEN AND BROCCOLI

1 tablespoon butter
4 to 5 boneless, skinless chicken breasts
2 cups broccoli florets
1 cup chicken broth
Juice from 1 lemon

Melt butter in a 9x13-inch baking dish by placing in preheated oven for 1 to 2 minutes. Add chicken and broccoli. Add chicken broth and lemon juice. Bake uncovered for 35 to 40 minutes at 400 degrees.

FRENCH SAUSAGE CASSOULET

½ cup carrots, chopped
½ cup red onion, chopped
1 teaspoon finely chopped fresh garlic
2 tablespoons butter
2 (15 ounce) cans great northern beans, rinsed and drained
¼ pound kielbasa, cut into ¼-inch slices
1 (8 ounce) can tomato sauce
½ teaspoon thyme
¼ cup butter cracker crumbs
3 tablespoons chopped fresh parsley

Sauté carrots, onion, and garlic with butter in a skillet. Combine onion mixture, beans, kielbasa, tomato sauce, and thyme in greased casserole dish. Sprinkle with cracker crumbs. Cover and bake for 35 to 45 minutes at 350 degrees. Sprinkle with parsley.

CRUNCHY TACOS

1 pound ground beef
1 tablespoon chili powder
1 cup salsa
8 taco shells
1 cup shredded lettuce
1 cup shredded cheddar cheese
Additional salsa
Sour cream

Cook beef and chili powder in skillet until browned. Drain. Add salsa and heat through.

Spoon about ¼ cup meat mixture into each taco. Top with lettuce and cheese. Serve with additional salsa and sour cream.

CREAMY ITALIAN CHICKEN

4 small boneless, skinless chicken breasts
Flour, to coat chicken breasts
1 tablespoon olive oil
¾ cup chicken broth
4 ounces cream cheese, cubed
2 tablespoons Italian dressing
Buttered noodles or rice

Lightly coat chicken breasts with flour. In a large skillet, add chicken to oil and cook for 5 to 6 minutes on each side until done. Remove chicken and reserve drippings. Add broth to drippings and stir. Add cream cheese and Italian dressing. Cook for 3 minutes until cream cheese is melted, stirring constantly with whisk. Return chicken to skillet and coat with sauce. Cook 2 more minutes. Serve with hot buttered noodles or rice.

ITALIAN CHICKEN AND RICE BAKE

¾ cup uncooked rice
¾ cup water
¾ cup milk
1 (10 ounce) can cream of mushroom soup
1 (16 ounce) package frozen vegetables
2 tablespoons grated Parmesan cheese
2 tablespoons dried Italian bread crumbs
2 tablespoons dijon mustard
2 tablespoons melted butter
4 boneless, skinless chicken breasts

Combine rice, water, milk, soup, and vegetables into 9x13-inch greased baking dish. In a separate large bowl, combine cheese and bread crumbs. Mix mustard with melted butter. Dip each chicken breast in mustard mixture and then in crumb mix. Place chicken on top of rice. Cover and bake for 1 hour at 400 degrees. Uncover during the last 15 minutes.

QUICK CLEANUP

Use lemon juice to clean stainless steel
for a beautiful, spotless finish.
Use it to clean your pots and pans, teakettle, sink,
and any other stainless steel surface.

BEEF AND BROCCOLI SAUTÉ

1 tablespoon butter
¾ pound thin beef strips
1 small sweet onion, sliced
2 cups fresh broccoli florets
½ cup fresh mushrooms, sliced
1 (2 ounce) envelope dry brown gravy mix
1 cup water
¼ teaspoon pepper

In a large skillet, heat butter over medium-high heat. Add beef strips and onion and sauté for 3 to 4 minutes; add broccoli and mushrooms. In a separate bowl, combine gravy mix, water, and pepper. Pour over beef mixture. Stir and bring to a boil. Cover and simmer 5 to 8 minutes or until broccoli is tender.

BEEF AND CORN BREAD BAKE

I pound ground beef, browned
I teaspoon oregano
I cup salsa
I (8 ounce) can tomato sauce
I (16 ounce) can whole kernel corn, drained
½ cup shredded sharp cheddar cheese
I (8 ounce) package corn muffin mix,
prepared according to package directions

Brown beef with oregano. Drain beef and add salsa, tomato sauce, and corn. Heat for 3 to 4 minutes on medium high. Stir in cheese. Pour into baking dish. Prepare corn muffin mix according to package directions. Spread over meat mixture. Bake for 25 minutes at 375 degrees until topping is golden brown. Let stand 10 minutes before serving.

BEEF TACO BAKE

1 pound ground beef, browned and drained
1 small sweet onion, chopped
1 (10 ounce) can condensed tomato soup
1 cup salsa
½ cup water
8 corn tortillas, cut into 1-inch pieces
1 cup shredded cheddar cheese, divided

Brown ground beef and drain. Add onion, soup, salsa, water, and tortillas to beef. Add ½ cup cheese and mix well. Spoon into 2-quart baking dish and cover. Bake at 400 degrees for 30 minutes. Sprinkle with remaining cheese.

FAST AND
FESTIVE MEALS

Give thanks to the Lord, for he is good!
His faithful love endures forever.
PSALM 118:1

BUENO TACO SALAD

1 (2 ounce) envelope taco seasoning
1 pound ground beef, browned
1 (16 ounce) bottle french dressing
1 medium-sized head of iceberg lettuce, chopped
2 large tomatoes, chopped
1 large green bell pepper, chopped
4 cups cheesy nacho chips, crushed
½ cup sour cream
½ cup sliced black olives

Mix taco seasoning with beef according to package directions. Let cool.
Mix seasoned beef with dressing, lettuce, tomatoes, pepper, and chips.
Top with sour cream and sliced black olives and serve immediately.

FIESTA FISH

1 pound frozen haddock or cod fillets, thawed
1 medium zucchini, sliced
1 medium yellow squash, sliced
1¼ cups thick and chunky salsa, divided
½ cup finely shredded mozzarella cheese

Cut fish into 4 pieces. Mix zucchini, squash, and 1 cup of salsa in a 9-inch square baking dish. Top with fish. Spoon 1 tablespoon remaining salsa over each piece of fish. Bake at 400 degrees for 15 minutes. Sprinkle each piece of fish with cheese. Bake an additional 8 to 12 minutes or until cheese is melted and fish is done.

PENNE AND SHRIMP DINNER

1 pound raw shrimp, peeled, deveined
1 teaspoon kosher salt
¼ teaspoon pepper
3 tablespoons olive oil
2 garlic cloves, minced
6 plum tomatoes, sliced thin
¼ cup chopped fresh cilantro, divided
3 tablespoons lime juice
6 ounces baby spinach leaves
12 ounces multigrain penne pasta, cooked
3 tablespoons water

Sprinkle shrimp with salt and pepper. Add oil, shrimp, and garlic to skillet and sauté for 2 minutes. Add tomatoes, half of the cilantro, and lime juice. Sauté for 3 minutes or until shrimp is no longer transparent. Add spinach and pasta. Add water and stir. Top with remaining cilantro and serve.

Invite your kids to help you measure and add in
the ingredients while you manage the hot oven.
It's a win-win situation. They'll be proud
of their creation and you'll enjoy the
quality time spent with your kids!

SALMON CAKES

½ cup fine bread crumbs
1 stalk celery, very finely chopped
2 tablespoons mayonnaise
2 tablespoons onion, diced fine
1 tablespoon parsley flakes
1 teaspoon lemon pepper seasoning
1 teaspoon baking powder
1 egg, beaten
1 (16 ounce) can pink salmon, drained and deboned
Baby spinach

Place all ingredients except salmon and spinach in a large bowl and mix well. Add salmon and mix gently but thoroughly. Shape into 4 patties. Place patties on lightly greased broiler pan and broil, 4 minutes on each side, 8 inches from source of heat. Serve with baby spinach.

YUMMY GUMBO

½ pound sliced smoked sausage, browned
2 (14 ounce) cans diced tomatoes, undrained
2 tablespoons cajun seasoning
1 (10 ounce) package frozen mixed vegetables, thawed
½ pound cooked shrimp
Cooked rice

Add all ingredients to skillet except shrimp and rice. Cook for 4 to 5 minutes. Stir in shrimp. Heat for 3 minutes just until shrimp is hot. Serve with rice.

SWEET AND SPICY PORK DINNER

1 pound pork tenderloin
¼ cup french dressing, divided
½ teaspoon chili powder
¼ teaspoon dry mustard
¼ teaspoon paprika
¼ teaspoon thyme
1 tablespoon honey
Cooked rice

Brush pork with 2 tablespoons french dressing. Mix dry ingredients and rub onto meat. Place in baking pan. Mix remaining 2 tablespoons dressing with honey and set aside. Bake at 425 degrees for 15 minutes. Brush with dressing/honey mixture. Bake an additional 10 minutes or until cooked through. Remove meat from oven and cover with foil. Let stand 5 minutes before slicing. Serve with rice.

ONE-DISH PORK DINNER

½ cup packed brown sugar
2 tablespoons butter, cut up
1 teaspoon ground cinnamon
6 pork boneless loin chops
1 small acorn squash, seeded, and cut into rings
1 large unpeeled red apple, cored and sliced

Mix brown sugar, butter, and cinnamon until crumbly; set aside. Place pork in 9x13-inch baking dish. Arrange squash and apples around pork. Sprinkle with brown sugar mixture. Bake at 350 degrees for 40 to 45 minutes or until squash is tender and pork is done.

ONE-POT TURKEY DINNER

1 pound turkey tenderloin
1 teaspoon salt
1/3 cup whole cranberries
1/2 cup orange juice
Dash pepper
1/3 cup walnuts, chopped
1 small onion, sliced
2 medium sweet potatoes, sliced
2 cups broccoli florets

Place turkey into roasting pan and sprinkle with salt. Combine cranberries, orange juice, pepper, and walnuts in a blender until just mixed. Spoon half of cranberry mixture on the turkey. Layer onion and sweet potato slices around turkey and cover with remaining cranberry mixture. Top with broccoli. Cover and bake at 450 degrees for 40 minutes or until done.

If your family is prone to distraction during dinnertime,
turn off the TV, leave the radio off,
don't answer the telephone. . . .
Make a "no interruptions" rule at the dinner table
so you can focus on just being together.

CRAB PRIMAVERA

1½ cups frozen vegetables
¼ cup water
1⅓ cups milk
¾ pound crabmeat
2 tablespoons butter
1 teaspoon garlic powder
¾ teaspoon dried basil
1½ cups instant white rice
1 cup mozzarella cheese

Bring vegetables and water to boil in medium saucepan, stirring occasionally. Reduce heat. Cover and simmer for 3 minutes. Add milk, crabmeat, butter, garlic powder, and basil. Bring to full boil. Stir in rice and cover. Remove from heat. Let stand 5 minutes. Fluff with fork and top with cheese.

PEPPER AND ZUCCHINI STIR-FRY

¼ cup olive oil
2 zucchini, sliced
½ cup cooked chicken, chopped
1 to 2 cloves fresh garlic
1 teaspoon salt
¼ teaspoon pepper
6 bell peppers of multi colors, washed and cut into strips
1 cup mozzarella cheese
Cooked rice

Heat oil and sauté zucchini and chicken for 4 to 5 minutes until lightly browned. Stir in garlic, salt, and pepper and cook for 1 minute. Add bell peppers and sauté. Remove from heat and add cheese. Serve with rice.

CRANBERRY GLAZED HAM DINNER

2 oranges, sliced
5 pounds fully cooked ham
¼ cup whole cloves
4 small red potatoes, pierced with fork
½ cup brown sugar
2 tablespoons honey
½ cup cranberry juice cocktail
1 tablespoon dry mustard
¼ teaspoon nutmeg

Arrange orange slices on ham in roasting pan. Press cloves into ham surface. Place potatoes around ham. Bake at 325 degrees for 90 minutes. Mix together brown sugar, honey, cranberry juice, mustard, and nutmeg. During the last 40 minutes, brush ham with mixture.

DESSERTS
AND SNACKS

How sweet your words taste to me;
they are sweeter than honey.
PSALM 119:103

NUTRITIOUS NO-BAKE COOKIES

½ cup peanut butter
½ cup honey
¼ cup orange juice
1½ cups nonfat dry milk
4 cups crispy rice cereal

Mix together peanut butter, honey, orange juice, and nonfat dry milk.
Add crispy rice cereal, mixing gently till coated. Shape into walnut-sized
balls.

GAMMY'S PEANUT BUTTER PIE

⅓ cup peanut butter
¾ cup powdered sugar
1 (9 inch) baked pie shell
1 large box of vanilla pudding (not instant),
prepared according to package directions
2 cups whipped topping

In a small bowl, use a pastry blender to combine peanut butter and powdered sugar and set aside. Line a baked pie shell with one-third of the peanut butter mixture. Make 1 large box of vanilla pudding and place it on top of peanut butter mixture. Chill to cool. Top with 2 cups whipped topping and sprinkle remaining peanut butter mixture over the entire top of the pie. Chill well.

SNACK KABOBS

1 large apple, sliced
5 strawberries, sliced
2 bananas, sliced
$\frac{1}{2}$ cup orange juice
Thin pretzel sticks

Dip fruit into orange juice to prevent browning and skewer onto thin pretzel sticks.

FROSTING IN A FLASH

Need frosting but don't have time to make any?
Sprinkle a bag of milk chocolate chips on top
while the cake or brownies are still warm.
Let it sit for 2 to 3 minutes.
The chips will melt and then you can spread the topping.

HEALTHY SNACK COOKIES

1 banana
1 cup crunchy peanut butter
½ cup white sugar
½ cup brown sugar, packed
2 eggs
1 cup whole wheat flour
1 cup white flour
1 teaspoon baking soda
1 cup quick oats
1 cup raisins or chocolate chips

Mix banana, peanut butter, and sugars until smooth. Mix in eggs. Add flours and baking soda and mix until just blended. Stir in oats and raisins or chocolate chips. Bake at 300 degrees for 10 to 15 minutes or until golden brown.

FROZEN YOGURT WAFFLES

2 frozen whole wheat waffles
½ cup frozen yogurt

Spread frozen yogurt between 2 waffles, creating a sandwich. Make ahead and freeze for a cool, healthy snack.

BANANA POPS

6 popsicle sticks
3 bananas, peeled and halved
½ cup peanut butter
¼ cup crispy rice cereal

Push a popsicle stick through the cut end of each banana. Spread peanut butter on the bananas and roll them in the cereal. Wrap them in waxed paper and freeze for 3 hours before serving.

TUNA SHELLS

8 jumbo pasta shells, cooked and drained
1 cup tuna salad
½ cup grated cheddar cheese

Fill each shell with tuna salad and sprinkle with cheese. Store in the refrigerator. Makes a great after-school snack.

CHEESY CRESCENT DOGS

1 (8 ounce) tube refrigerated crescent rolls
4 reduced-fat hot dogs, cut in half
4 slices cheddar cheese

Unroll crescent dough. Add a hot dog and one-half slice of cheese to each roll. Roll up and pinch seams. Place on a greased baking sheet. Bake as crescent package instructs.

KRISTY'S TRIPLE CHIP WONDER COOKIES

1 box white cake mix
1 stick butter, melted
2 eggs
½ cup white chocolate chips
½ cup butterscotch chips
½ cup semisweet chocolate chips

Combine cake mix with melted butter and eggs. Stir in chips. Drop by spoonful onto ungreased cookie sheet. Bake for 6 to 7 minutes at 350 degrees. Oven times may vary depending on your oven. Don't overcook; the cookies will set up as they cool.

COOKIES FOR LATER

Double your cookie recipe and
store extra dough in waxed paper.
Keep the dough handy in your refrigerator
to slice and bake when needed.

PIZZA BREAD STICKS

1 (13.8 ounce) tube refrigerated pizza crust
1 tablespoon butter, melted
1 teaspoon garlic salt
¼ teaspoon oregano
1 (8 ounce) jar prepared pizza sauce

Cut pizza dough into strips. Place on a greased cookie sheet and brush with melted butter. Sprinkle with garlic salt and oregano. Bake at 350 degrees for 12 to 15 minutes or until golden brown. Serve warm with pizza sauce.

PEANUT BUTTER BALLS

½ cup crunchy peanut butter
½ cup bran flakes
½ cup graham crackers, crushed

Mix peanut butter and bran flakes in a bowl. Shape into balls and roll in graham crackers.

OATMEAL KISS FREEZER COOKIES

1 cup butter, softened (no substitutions)
1 cup powdered sugar
1 teaspoon vanilla
1¼ cups flour
1 cup quick oats
⅛ teaspoon salt
1 small bag chocolate kiss candies, unwrapped

Cream together butter, sugar, and vanilla. Stir in flour, oats, and salt. Shape dough into two long rolls, each 1½ inches in diameter. Wrap in waxed paper. Chill for at least 2 hours or freeze for up to 3 months. When ready to bake, cut dough into ¼-inch slices and place on cookie sheet. Top each with a chocolate kiss. Bake at 350 degrees for 10 to 12 minutes or until golden brown.

EASY ROLL-UPS

1 (8 ounce) package cream cheese, softened
1 cup light sour cream
1 cup finely grated cheddar cheese
1 (4 ounce) can chopped black olives
2 tablespoons ranch dressing
1 teaspoon salt
10 flour tortillas
Salsa (optional)

Mix all ingredients except tortillas and salsa thoroughly. Spread ⅛ cup of mixture on each tortilla. Roll tightly and wrap in plastic wrap. Cover and refrigerate for at least 2 hours. Slice. Serve with salsa if desired.

EASY SWEET POTATO FRIES

2 tablespoons frozen orange juice concentrate, thawed
1 teaspoon onion powder
½ teaspoon salt
¼ teaspoon pepper
½ teaspoon cinnamon
1 pound sweet potatoes, cut into ½-inch sticks

Line a cookie sheet with foil and spray with cooking spray. Combine all ingredients except potatoes. Mix well. Add potato sticks and mix to coat. Arrange sticks on foil in a single layer. Bake at 425 degrees for 30 minutes, turning every 10 minutes.

EASY HOMEMADE APPLESAUCE

4 Red Delicious apples, peeled, cored, and chopped
4 Granny Smith apples, peeled, cored, and chopped
1 ½ cups water
½ cup white sugar
1 teaspoon ground cinnamon

In a large saucepan, combine apples, water, sugar, and cinnamon. Cover and cook over medium heat for 15 to 20 minutes or until apples are soft. Allow to cool, then mash with a fork or potato masher.

CHEESE AND VEGGIE MELT

4 slices whole wheat bread
1 small sweet onion, finely chopped
1 medium tomato, diced
1 green bell pepper, finely chopped
1 cup shredded cheddar cheese
¼ teaspoon seasoned salt

Lay bread slices on baking sheet. Mix remaining ingredients together. Top each slice of bread with one-fourth of mixture, spreading to the edges. Broil for 3 to 5 minutes on low until cheese melts. Watch closely to prevent burning.

SAUCEPAN COOKIES

½ cup skim milk
2 cups sugar
3 tablespoons unsweetened cocoa powder
½ cup butter (no substitutions)
3 tablespoons crunchy peanut butter
3 cups quick oats
1 teaspoon vanilla extract

In a saucepan, combine milk, sugar, cocoa, butter, and peanut butter. Stir and bring to boil over medium heat. Let boil for 1½ minutes but do not stir. Remove from heat. Stir in oats and vanilla. Drop by teaspoon onto waxed paper. Cool.

NO-STICK DOUGH

To keep dough from sticking to your rolling pin,
try using nylon. Take a clean, never-worn knee-high stocking
and cut off the toe. Slide the nylon over your rolling pin.
The nylon helps hold an even layer of flour on the pin
so you can easily flatten moist dough.

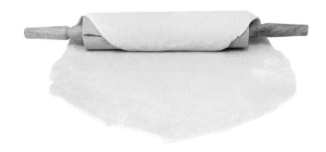

LEMON BARS

1 (18 ounce) box lemon cake mix with pudding
1 egg
½ cup vegetable oil
1 (8 ounce) package cream cheese
¼ cup sugar
1 tablespoon lemon juice

Combine cake mix, egg, and oil. Mix well. Reserve one cup of mixture for the topping and press the rest into an ungreased 9x13-inch pan with a fork. Bake at 350 degrees for 15 minutes. Cool. In a medium bowl, beat cream cheese, sugar, and lemon juice until smooth. Spread evenly over crust. Crumble the reserved cake mix over the top. Bake for 15 minutes or until filling is set. Cool and serve.

FRUIT PIZZA

1 (20 ounce) package refrigerated sugar cookie dough
1 (8 ounce) package cream cheese, softened
⅓ cup sugar
½ teaspoon vanilla
Assorted fresh fruit, sliced
½ cup raspberry preserves
2 tablespoons cold water

Press cookie dough into a round or rectangular pizza pan. Bake at 375 degrees for 12 minutes or until golden brown. Cool. Meanwhile, beat cream cheese, sugar, and vanilla until smooth. Spread over crust. Arrange fruit on top of cream cheese layer. Mix preserves and water and spoon over fruit. Refrigerate before serving.

FROZEN PUMPKIN DESSERT

1 (8 ounce) package cream cheese, softened
½ cup sugar
¼ cup brown sugar
1 (16 ounce) can pumpkin
1 teaspoon pumpkin pie spice
1 (8 ounce) tub whipped topping, thawed, divided

Beat cream cheese and sugars until well blended. Add pumpkin and spice. Mix well. Reserve ½ cup of whipped topping. Gently add remaining whipped topping. Pour into 9-inch square baking dish. Freeze 4 hours or until firm. Top with reserved whipped topping.

QUICK CAKE MIX COOKIES

½ cup butter, softened
3 ounces cream cheese, softened
1 egg
1 (18 ounce) box devil's food cake mix
1½ cups semisweet chocolate chips, divided

Beat together butter, cream cheese, and egg. Add cake mix and beat well. Stir in 1 cup chocolate chips. Roll dough into balls and place on ungreased cookie sheet. Press down on each ball with palm to flatten. Bake at 375 degrees for 7 to 9 minutes. Cool for 2 minutes then remove from cookie sheets to cool completely. Melt remaining chocolate chips and drizzle over cooled cookies.

EASY MICROWAVE FUDGE

2 cups semisweet chocolate chips
1 cup milk chocolate chips
1 (14 ounce) can sweetened condensed milk
1 teaspoon vanilla

In a large microwavable bowl, combine chocolate chips and sweetened condensed milk. Microwave on high for 2 minutes. Add vanilla. Stir. Line an 8-inch square pan with waxed paper and pour in fudge. Refrigerate.

CHOCOLATE ICE CREAM BALLS

3 cups chocolate ice cream
1½ cups semisweet chocolate chips
15 chocolate sandwich cookies, crushed
½ cup milk chocolate chips, melted

Mix ice cream and semisweet chocolate chips. Using an ice cream scoop, scoop ice cream mixture into six balls. Roll in crushed cookies. Place on cookie sheet lined with waxed paper and freeze for 2 hours or until firm. Place frozen ice cream balls on a wire rack. Spoon melted chocolate over each ball. Freeze again until firm, at least 1 hour. Remove from freezer 10 minutes before serving.

STRAWBERRY CREAM CHEESE CRESCENTS

1 (8 count) tube refrigerated crescent rolls
8 tablespoons cream cheese
8 teaspoons strawberry preserves

Unroll crescent rolls and fill each with 1 tablespoon cream cheese and 1 teaspoon strawberry preserves. Roll. Bake according to package directions. Allow to cool before serving.

CHILI AND CHEESE

1 pound ground beef
1 small onion, chopped
2 tablespoons chili seasoning
1 can condensed tomato soup
½ cup water
2 eggs, slightly beaten
1 cup milk
2 cups corn chips, crushed
1 cup shredded Monterey Jack cheese
1 cup sour cream
½ cup shredded sharp cheddar cheese

Brown beef with onion. Drain. Combine beef, onion, chili seasoning, soup, and water in a large skillet. Simmer 5 minutes. Add eggs and milk. Cook and stir until bubbly. Add corn chips and monterey jack cheese. Pour into a casserole dish. Bake at 350 degrees for 35 minutes. Top with sour cream and cheddar cheese during last 5 minutes of cooking.

PICNIC SALAD

1 to 2 cups lettuce, finely chopped
1 stalk celery, finely sliced
2 carrots, shredded
1 sweet onion, sliced thin
1 cucumber, sliced thin
1 cup mayonnaise
8 slices bacon, cooked and crumbled
1 cup sharp cheddar cheese, shredded

Line bottom of 9-inch square pan with lettuce. Layer remaining vegetables on top in order given. Spread mayonnaise over the top. Sprinkle bacon and cheese over mayonnaise.

GLAZED HAM LOAF DINNER

1 pound ground pork
1 pound ground ham
10 butter crackers, crushed
2 eggs
1¼ cups milk
1 teaspoon dry mustard
4 red potatoes, pierced with fork

Sauce:
⅓ cup crushed pineapple
½ cup brown sugar
½ teaspoon dry mustard
¼ cup water

Mix pork, ham, cracker crumbs, eggs, milk, and mustard. Form into loaf and place in roasting pan. Surround with potatoes. Combine sauce ingredients and pour over loaf. Bake at 350 degrees for 1½ hours.

APRICOT CHICKEN DINNER

5 to 6 boneless, skinless chicken breasts
4 red potatoes, pricked with fork
1 cup baby carrots
1 (16 ounce) bottle Russian dressing
1 cup mayonnaise
1 cup apricot jam
2 envelopes onion soup mix

Place chicken in flat baking pan. Surround chicken with potatoes and carrots. Mix remaining ingredients and pour over chicken and vegetables. Bake at 350 degrees for 1 hour or until chicken is done and veggies are tender.

CHICKEN SALAD LOG

1 (8 ounce) package cream cheese
1/4 cup mayonnaise
2 tablespoons lemon juice
1/2 teaspoon salt
1/8 teaspoon ground pepper
Dash hot sauce
2 cups finely chopped cooked chicken
2 hard-boiled eggs, chopped fine
1/4 cup sweet onion, diced fine
Olives
Toast or crackers

Mix together cream cheese, mayonnaise, lemon juice, salt, pepper, and hot sauce. Stir in chopped chicken, eggs, and onion. Shape into log. Wrap in plastic wrap. Refrigerate 4 hours or overnight. Garnish with olives and serve with toast or crackers.

PARTY STYLE EGG BAKE

1 pound bulk pork sausage, cooked and crumbled
½ cup sweet onion, chopped
2 tomatoes, chopped
2 cups shredded mozzarella cheese
1¼ cups buttermilk baking mix
12 eggs
1 cup milk
1 teaspoon salt
½ teaspoon pepper

Layer sausage, onions, tomatoes, and cheese in greased 9x13-inch baking dish. Beat remaining ingredients; pour over sausage mixture. Cook at 350 degrees for 30 minutes or until golden brown and set. Cut into squares.

BACON IN A FLASH

Cook up a pound of bacon until done but not crisp.
When cooled and drained of fat, cut or crumble
the bacon and store it in a freezer container.
It can then be added quickly to a casserole or salad.

FAJITAS

2 to 3 boneless, skinless chicken breasts, cut into strips
2 tablespoons oil
1 green pepper, cut into strips
1 red bell pepper, cut into strips
1 small sweet onion, sliced
10 to 12 flour tortillas
1 cup salsa (optional)
1 cup shredded cheddar cheese (optional)
½ cup sour cream (optional)

Sauté chicken in oil in a large skillet for 4 minutes. Add peppers and onion; cook over low heat for 5 minutes or until tender. Put mixture into tortillas. Top with salsa, cheese, and sour cream, if desired.

FAMILY FISH DINNER

2 pounds white fish fillets
½ cup french dressing
1½ cups crushed butter crackers
2 tablespoons butter, melted
Dash paprika
French fries
Coleslaw

Skin fillets and cut into equal portions. Dip fish into dressing and roll in cracker crumbs to coat. Place on greased cookie sheet. Drizzle butter over fish. Sprinkle with paprika. Bake at 500 degrees for 10 to 12 minutes or until fish flakes easily. Serve with french fries and coleslaw.

GRILLED KABOBS

1 cup ketchup
1 teaspoon salt
2 tablespoons steak sauce
2 tablespoons Worcestershire sauce
1 tablespoon sugar
2 tablespoons apple cider vinegar
2 tablespoons olive oil
¼ cup water
Steak, cut into cubes
Boneless, skinless chicken, cut into cubes
Sliced vegetables

Mix all ingredients in a saucepan except meat and vegetables. Bring to a boil. Pour over meat. Marinate in refrigerate 2 hours or overnight. Alternate on skewer with your favorite vegetables. Grill over medium heat, basting with leftover marinade.

ITALIAN MEATBALL SOUP

1 pound frozen fully cooked meatballs
1 (16 ounce) jar spaghetti sauce
1 teaspoon oregano
2½ cups water
1 (20 ounce) package frozen cheese tortellini
½ cup grated Parmesan cheese

In large pot, combine meatballs, sauce, oregano, and water. Bring to a boil. Reduce heat, stir in tortellini and simmer for 10 minutes or until meatballs and pasta are tender. Sprinkle with Parmesan cheese.

PARTY STYLE CHEF'S SALAD

Dressing:
2 tablespoons apple cider vinegar
1 tablespoon ketchup
4 tablespoons olive oil
¼ teaspoon salt
¼ teaspoon fresh ground black pepper

Salad:
1 head romaine lettuce
2 cooked chicken breasts, cut into strips
1 tomato, sliced
2 hard-boiled eggs, sliced
12 whole black olives
1 ripe avocado, cubed
1 red bell pepper, chopped

Mix dressing ingredients and chill. Tear lettuce into 2-inch pieces and place in mixing bowl. Add remaining ingredients. Pour dressing over salad. Toss gently and serve.

SPINACH RAVIOLI

2 cups water
1 (10 ounce) package frozen creamed spinach
1 (24 ounce) package frozen cheese ravioli
1 (16 ounce) jar alfredo sauce
½ cup shredded Parmesan cheese

Boil water in a large pot. Add spinach pouch and return to boil. Boil for 3 minutes. Add ravioli, return to boil. Reduce heat and simmer 5 minutes until ravioli float. Drain and remove spinach. Place spinach in a large skillet. Add alfredo sauce and mix gently. Cook over medium heat for 5 minutes until the mixture just begins to bubble, stirring frequently. Add ravioli and stir. Sprinkle with cheese prior to serving.

BAYOU CASSEROLE

½ cup chopped green pepper
1 cup chopped celery
½ cup chopped onion
2 tablespoons butter
2 pounds fresh cooked shrimp
1 pound fresh cooked scallops
1 cup cooked rice
1 small jar pimentos, drained and chopped
¾ cup half-and-half
1 can mushroom soup
1 cup mayonnaise
1 tablespoon Worcestershire sauce
Dash white pepper

Sauté green pepper, celery, and onion in butter. Toss all ingredients together and put in buttered baking dish. Cook uncovered at 375 degrees for 35 minutes or until heated through.

CHICKEN POTPIE

1 (10 ounce) can cream of chicken soup
1 (9 ounce) package frozen mixed vegetables, thawed
2 (5 ounce) cans chunk chicken breast
½ cup milk
1 egg
1 cup all-purpose baking mix
1 teaspoon seasoned salt

Mix soup, vegetables, and chicken in 9-inch pie plate. In a separate bowl, mix milk, egg, baking mix, and seasoned salt. Pour over chicken mixture. Bake for 30 minutes at 400 degrees or until golden brown.

CHICKEN NACHO SALAD

1 tablespoon vegetable oil
1 pound boneless, skinless chicken breasts, cut into strips
1 (16 ounce) can corn, drained
1 (15 ounce) can tomato sauce
1 (4 ounce) can diced green chilies
1 teaspoon chili powder
1 teaspoon onion powder
Tortilla chips
3 cups shredded lettuce
1 cup shredded cheddar cheese

In large skillet, heat oil over medium heat. Add chicken and cook for 5 minutes. Stir in corn, tomato sauce, chilies, chili powder, and onion powder. Heat to a boil, reduce heat to medium, and cook for 10 minutes, stirring occasionally. Layer tortilla chips and lettuce in a separate bowl. Spoon chicken mixture onto lettuce and top with cheese.

BEEF AND NOODLES

½ pound lean ground beef
1 onion, chopped
1 (15 ounce) can chili, no beans
1 (10 ounce) can diced tomatoes with green chilies, drained
1 tablespoon mustard
1 cup cooked elbow macaroni
1 egg, beaten
½ cup shredded cheddar cheese
Additional cheese (optional)

In large skillet, cook ground beef and onion until beef is browned; drain. Stir in chili, tomatoes with green chilies, and mustard. Bring to a boil. Reduce heat and simmer 10 minutes. Remove from heat and add remaining ingredients. Stir and pour into casserole dish. Bake uncovered for 35 to 40 minutes at 350 degrees. Sprinkle with additional cheese if desired.

CHEESY CHICKEN AND BROCCOLI

2 (12 ounce) jars chicken gravy
1 tablespoon lemon juice
2 cups frozen broccoli florets, thawed
2 cups cooked chicken, cubed
1 (10 ounce) package frozen puff pastry shells, baked
½ cup shredded cheddar cheese

Mix gravy, lemon juice, broccoli, and chicken in saucepan. Heat through. Serve in pastry shells. Sprinkle with cheese.

CHEESE AND CHICKEN ENCHILADAS

1 small onion, chopped
1 tablespoon butter
1½ cups cooked, shredded chicken breast meat
4 ounces cream cheese
¾ cup shredded cheddar cheese, divided
1 cup salsa, divided
8 flour tortillas

Sauté onion in butter. Add chicken, cream cheese, ½ cup cheddar cheese, and ¾ cup salsa. Heat and stir until cheeses are melted. Spoon ⅓ cup of the mixture onto each tortilla. Roll up and place in a lightly greased 9x13-inch baking dish. Spread remaining salsa over tortillas and top with remaining cheese. Cover and bake for 15 to 20 minutes at 350 degrees.

CREAMY HAM CASSEROLE

2 cups frozen broccoli florets, thawed
1½ cups coarsely chopped ham
1½ cups rotini pasta, cooked and drained
½ cup mayonnaise
½ green bell pepper, chopped
¼ cup milk
1 teaspoon salt
¼ teaspoon pepper
1½ cups cheddar cheese, divided
¼ cup seasoned croutons

Mix all ingredients except ½ cup of cheese and croutons. Place in a casserole dish. Sprinkle with reserved cheese. Bake for 30 minutes at 350 degrees. Sprinkle with seasoned croutons during the last 5 minutes of baking.

GERM-FREE SPONGES

Keep sponges fresh and disinfected by washing them
in the top rack of your dishwasher.

CHICKEN AND RICE BAKE

1 (10 ounce) can cream of mushroom soup
1⅓ cups water
¾ cup uncooked instant white rice
¼ teaspoon salt
⅛ teaspoon pepper
4 skinless, boneless chicken breasts
Dash paprika

Mix soup, water, rice, salt, and pepper in a shallow baking dish. Place chicken on rice mixture. Sprinkle with paprika. Cover and bake at 375 degrees for 45 minutes or until chicken is no longer pink and rice is done.

CHICKEN SKILLET

4 cups frozen hash brown potatoes, diced
1 cup onion, chopped
½ cup green bell pepper, chopped
½ cup red bell pepper, chopped
2 cups cooked chicken, cubed
3 tablespoons oil
1 cup half-and-half
2 chicken bouillon cubes
2 teaspoons flour
¼ teaspoon pepper
1 cup shredded sharp cheddar cheese

Cook potatoes, onion, and bell peppers in a large skillet with oil for 13 minutes or until potatoes are cooked. Sprinkle chicken over potatoes. In small saucepan, combine oil, half-and-half, chicken bouillon cubes, flour, and pepper. Cook for 4 minutes over medium heat, stirring constantly until mixture thickens. Pour over chicken. Top with cheese.

CHEESY TACO CASSEROLE

1 pound lean ground beef
1 small onion, chopped
1 (16 ounce) jar salsa
1 (10 ounce) can red enchilada sauce
12 taco shells, broken into pieces
1½ cups shredded cheddar cheese, divided

Brown beef in skillet with onion. Drain and return to skillet. Add salsa and enchilada sauce to beef and onion. Bring to a boil. Reduce heat to low; cook, stirring frequently, for 4 minutes. Layer half of taco pieces in ungreased 9x13-inch baking dish. Top with half of beef mixture and half of cheese. Repeat layers once. Bake for 15 minutes at 350 degrees.

CREAMY CHICKEN CASSEROLE

2 tablespoons butter
¼ cup celery, chopped fine
1 cup fresh mushrooms, sliced
½ cup sweet onion, chopped
1 cup sour cream
¾ cup milk
2 (5 ounce) cans chunk breast of chicken, drained and flaked
1 cup frozen peas
8 ounces egg noodles, cooked and drained
¼ cup grated Parmesan cheese

In saucepan, cook celery, mushrooms, and onion in butter until tender. Stir in sour cream, milk, chicken, peas, and noodles. Pour into a casserole dish. Sprinkle cheese over the top. Bake for 25 minutes at 350 degrees.

POTPIE

1 pound ground beef, browned and drained
1/4 cup chopped onion
1 (10 ounce) package frozen peas and carrots, thawed
1 cup cooked potatoes, chopped
2 cups cheddar cheese
2 tablespoons butter
2 tablespoons flour
1/2 teaspoon salt
1 cup water
1 (8 ounce) can refrigerated crescent rolls

Place beef, onion, peas and carrots, potatoes, and cheese into 9-inch square baking dish. In a saucepan, add flour and salt to butter; whisk and cook for 2 minutes. Add water and bring to boil, stirring constantly. Simmer on low for 3 minutes. Pour over all. Unroll dough and place on top, covering entire surface. Bake at 375 degrees for 25 minutes.

EASY BEAN ENCHILADAS

1 (16 ounce) jar salsa
1 (16 ounce) can refried beans
1 (10 ounce) can red enchilada sauce
½ cup sliced black olives
10 corn tortillas, sliced in half, divided
2 cups shredded cheddar cheese, divided

In a saucepan, bring salsa, beans, enchilada sauce, and olives to a boil.
Reduce heat to low and cook for 5 minutes, stirring constantly. Layer
half of tortillas on the bottom of greased 9x13-inch baking dish. Cover
with half of bean mix; sprinkle with 1 cup cheese. Repeat layers once.
Bake, covered, for 25 minutes at 375 degrees. Remove cover during last
5 minutes.

PEPPER STEAK STIR-FRY

½ cup steak sauce
¼ cup soy sauce
1½ tablespoons cornstarch
1 pound beef top round steak, sliced thin
1 tablespoon oil
1 green bell pepper, cut into strips
1 small sweet onion, sliced
¾ cup beef broth
Cooked rice

Mix steak sauce, soy sauce, and cornstarch; coat meat and drain, reserving sauce. Cook and stir meat in hot oil in large skillet for 3 minutes. Add pepper and onion; cook 1 minute. Add beef broth and reserved sauce; bring to boil. Reduce heat; simmer 1 minute. Serve with rice.

APPLE PEANUT BUTTER ROLLS

4 slices white bread, crusts removed
½ cup peanut butter
¼ cup apple butter
¼ cup shredded apples

Roll each slice of bread with a rolling pin until flat. Spread two tablespoons of peanut butter on each slice of bread. Top each slice with one tablespoon of apple butter and one tablespoon shredded apples. Roll up sandwiches and cut into bite-sized pieces.

ITALIAN SAUSAGE SANDWICH

2 tablespoons butter
1 small sweet onion, sliced
1 green bell pepper, sliced
1 red bell pepper, sliced
6 to 8 precooked sausage links
Hot dog buns
Provolone cheese

Sauté onion and peppers in butter. Add sausage links and heat until warmed through. Place 2 sausage links in a hot dog bun. Add as many onions and peppers as you like. Top with 1 piece of provolone cheese. Place on a cookie sheet and broil on low until cheese is melted.

MEATBALL SUBS

3 meatballs, precooked and frozen
Hot dog bun
2 tablespoons spaghetti sauce, warmed
Mozzarella cheese

Warm meatballs in microwave according to package directions. Put 3 meatballs in 1 hot dog bun. Top with warm sauce and top with cheese.

BANANA APPLE PB & J

2 tablespoons peanut butter
2 slices whole wheat bread
1 tablespoon strawberry preserves
1 small banana, sliced
1 tablespoon minced apple

Spread peanut butter on 1 slice of bread and top with preserves, banana, and minced apple. Top with remaining slice of bread. Cut in half and serve.

QUICK CHICKEN QUESADILLAS

1 flour tortilla
2½ ounces chunk chicken
1 tablespoon red bell pepper, chopped
1 teaspoon diced green onion
1 slice American cheese

Top tortilla with chicken, pepper, onion, and cheese. Fold in half.
Microwave on high for 15 to 20 seconds or until cheese is melted.

CHICKEN PASTA SALAD

6 ounces multicolored pasta noodles, cooked, drained, and rinsed
1 celery stalk, chopped
1 carrot, chopped
1 green onion, chopped
6 to 8 cherry tomatoes, cut in half
¼ cup sliced black olives
2 baked, boneless, skinless chicken breasts, chopped
¼ cup Parmesan cheese
½ cup Italian dressing

Mix all ingredients together and serve.

EGG SALAD

5 to 6 hard-boiled eggs, chopped
¼ cup celery, chopped
¼ cup onion, chopped
¼ cup mayonnaise
1 tablespoon dry mustard
1 teaspoon sugar
1 teaspoon salt
½ teaspoon pepper
Lettuce or toast

Mix first 8 ingredients; serve on lettuce or toast.

It is said that a watched pot never boils—but an unattended pot can easily boil over and create a cleaning challenge. Try rubbing butter around the inside top inch or two of your pot to prevent boiled-over mishaps.

GRAPE CHICKEN SALAD

2 (5 ounce) cans chicken breast, drained
¼ cup mayonnaise
¼ cup sweet onion, chopped
6 to 8 red seedless grapes, cut in half
¼ cup chopped walnuts
1 teaspoon seasoned salt
Lettuce or toast

Mix first 6 ingredients; serve
on lettuce or toast.

HAM SALAD SANDWICHES

1 ½ pounds cooked ham, diced and trimmed
½ cup celery, sliced thin
2 tablespoons onion, diced fine
1 ¼ cups mayonnaise
1 tablespoon mustard
3 tablespoons sweet pickle relish
Salt and pepper to taste
Crackers or toast

Place half of the ham in a food processor and chop until ham salad consistency. Place in a bowl. Process the remaining ham and add to the bowl. Add the next 6 ingredients; spread on crackers or toast to serve.

TURKEY RANCH WRAPS

3 slices deli turkey
1 flour tortilla
½ cup shredded mozzarella cheese
1 cup lettuce
1 slice of tomato
1 tablespoon ranch dressing

Place turkey on tortilla and top with cheese. Cook in microwave for 1 minute until cheese is melted. Add lettuce and tomato. Spread ranch dressing on top. Roll and serve.

CHICKEN AND SPINACH SALAD

Dressing:
¼ cup olive oil
3 tablespoons apple cider vinegar
1 tablespoon sugar
1 tablespoon soy sauce
1 teaspoon dark sesame oil
½ teaspoon ginger

Salad:
1 (6 ounce) bag baby spinach
2 cups cooked chicken breast, cubed
1 (11 ounce) can mandarin oranges, drained
¼ cup green onions, sliced
¼ cup toasted slivered almonds

Combine dressing ingredients and chill for 1 hour. Gently toss all salad ingredients in large bowl. Add dressing and serve.

BACON CHILI SANDWICHES

6 slices bread
6 slices cheddar cheese
1 (15 ounce) can chili beans
6 slices bacon, cooked

Place bread on cookie sheet. Place one slice of cheese on each piece of bread. Add 4 tablespoons of chili beans on each piece of bread. Top each with a slice of bacon. Broil on low until cheese is melted.

WARM TUNA LUNCH

1 (6½ ounce) can albacore tuna, drained
4 ounces low-fat cream cheese
Toast
Fruit and vegetable slices

Mix tuna with cream cheese in a microwavable bowl. Microwave for 25 to 30 seconds. Spread on toast and serve with fruit and vegetable slices.

BACON AND CHEESE BREAKFAST PIZZA

1 (9 inch) refrigerated piecrust
½ pound bacon, cooked and crumbled
1 cup shredded cheddar cheese
4 eggs
12 ounces sour cream
1 teaspoon parsley

Roll crust to fit a 12-inch pizza pan. Bake at 425 degrees for 5 minutes. Sprinkle bacon and cheese evenly over crust. Beat eggs, sour cream, and parsley until smooth. Pour over pizza. Bake 20 to 25 minutes or until pizza is puffy and golden brown.

BREAKFAST SMOOTHIE

1 cup crushed ice
½ cup frozen orange juice concentrate
1 cup skim milk
1 medium banana
½ cup vanilla yogurt
1 tablespoon honey

Place ice in bottom of blender. Add
remaining ingredients. Puree until smooth.
Serve immediately.

BREAKFAST SKILLET

½ pound bulk pork sausage, browned and drained
2 cups frozen shredded hash browns
1 (10 ounce) can diced tomatoes and green chilies, drained
8 ounces processed American cheese, cubed
6 eggs
2 tablespoons water

Brown sausage and chilies and drain. Add hash browns and tomatoes to skillet used for browning sausage. Cook for 5 minutes then add cheese. In a separate bowl, whisk eggs and water together. Pour evenly over ingredients in skillet. Place skillet in oven. Bake for 20 minutes at 375 degrees or until egg mixture is set. Let stand 5 minutes before serving.

CHOCOLATE BANANA SMOOTHIE

1 cup crushed ice
2 large bananas
1 ½ cups milk
¼ cup vanilla yogurt
3 tablespoons chocolate instant breakfast mix

Place ice in bottom of blender. Add remaining ingredients. Puree until smooth. Serve immediately.

BANANA BARS

¾ cup butter, softened
1 cup brown sugar
1 egg
3 ripe bananas, mashed
½ teaspoon ground cinnamon
½ teaspoon salt
4 cups quick oats
½ cup raisins or chocolate chips

In a large mixing bowl, cream together the butter and sugar. Add egg, bananas, cinnamon, and salt. Mix well. Add remaining ingredients and mix. Spread into greased 9x13-inch pan. Bake for 45 to 50 minutes or until a toothpick comes out clean. Allow bars to cool before cutting into squares.

PUMPKIN PIE SMOOTHIE

1 cup crushed ice
½ cup pumpkin puree
½ cup pineapple chunks
1½ cups orange juice
½ cup vanilla yogurt
1 tablespoon brown sugar
1 whole graham cracker
½ teaspoon pumpkin pie spice
Dash cinnamon for garnish

Place ice in bottom of blender. Add remaining ingredients except cinnamon. Puree until smooth. Serve immediately with a sprinkle of cinnamon.

PUMPKIN FIBER MUFFINS

1 ½ cups flour
½ cup sugar
2 teaspoons baking powder
½ teaspoon baking soda
½ teaspoon salt
1 teaspoon cinnamon
2 eggs, beaten
1 cup canned pumpkin
1 cup bran cereal
¾ cup milk
½ cup light corn syrup
½ cup raisins

Combine all ingredients except raisins and blend well. Stir in raisins. Spoon into prepared muffin cups. Bake at 400 degrees for 18 to 20 minutes. Cool in pan for 5 minutes.

An egg slicer works great for slicing strawberries, mushrooms, boiled potatoes, cooked and peeled beets, and much more.

BAKED SAUSAGE CASSEROLE

12 slices white bread, cubed
1 pound ground sausage, cooked and drained
1 cup shredded cheddar cheese
6 eggs
2 cups milk
1 teaspoon salt
½ teaspoon pepper

Evenly spread bread cubes in a greased 9x13-inch pan. Spoon sausage over bread and top with cheese. In a separate bowl, beat eggs, milk, salt, and pepper. Pour over bread mixture. Bake at 350 degrees for 20 to 25 minutes or until done.

CHEESY HASH BROWN CASSEROLE

1 (32 ounce) bag frozen shredded hash browns
2 (10 ounce) cans potato soup
16 ounces sour cream
2 cups shredded sharp cheddar cheese
1 cup Parmesan cheese
¼ cup real bacon bits

Combine all ingredients; stir well. Spoon into greased 9x13-inch baking dish. Bake at 350 degrees for 40 minutes or until golden brown.

BREAKFAST PIZZA

1 (8 count) package refrigerated crescent rolls
1 pound ground sausage, cooked and drained
1 cup frozen hash browns, thawed
1 cup shredded sharp cheddar cheese
5 eggs
¼ cup milk
½ teaspoon salt
¼ teaspoon pepper

Press crescent dough in slightly greased 12-inch pizza pan. Seal perforations. Spoon sausage over dough. Sprinkle with potatoes. Top with cheddar cheese. In a bowl, beat together remaining ingredients. Pour on top. Bake at 375 degrees for 25 to 30 minutes.

STRAWBERRY CREAM CHEESE CREPES

⅔ cup milk
2 eggs
2 tablespoons sugar
6 tablespoons flour
2 tablespoons butter
4 teaspoons strawberry preserves
8 teaspoons cream cheese

In a blender, combine milk, eggs, sugar, and flour. Heat butter in small frying pan. Pour ¼ of batter into pan. Flip when edges are brown. Fill each crepe with 1 teaspoon strawberry preserves and 2 teaspoons cream cheese. Roll and serve.

BREAKFAST LASAGNA

½ cup sour cream
1 (10 ounce) can cream of mushroom soup
1 (32 ounce) bag frozen hash browns
1 sweet onion, diced
1 pound cooked bacon, diced
1 cup shredded cheddar cheese
1 cup shredded mozzarella cheese

Mix sour cream and mushroom soup until well blended. In a lasagna pan, layer hash browns, soup mixture, onion, bacon, and cheeses, in that order. Cover and bake at 325 degrees for 1 hour. Remove foil and bake an additional 5 minutes.

BACON AND POTATO CASSEROLE

4 cups frozen shredded hash browns
½ cup finely chopped onion
8 ounces bacon, cooked and crumbled
1 cup shredded cheddar cheese
1 (12 ounce) can evaporated milk
1 large egg, lightly beaten
¼ teaspoon pepper
1 teaspoon seasoned salt

Layer half the potatoes, half the onion, half the bacon, and half the cheese in greased 8-inch square baking dish; repeat layers. Combine evaporated milk, egg, pepper, and seasoned salt in small bowl. Pour evenly on top of layers. Cover and bake for 55 to 60 minutes at 350 degrees. Uncover and bake for 5 additional minutes. Let stand for 10 minutes before serving.

© 2010 by Barbour Publishing, Inc.

Compiled by MariLee Parrish.

ISBN 978-1-60260-743-9

Cover image: David Prince/Food Pix/Getty Images

Published by Barbour Publishing, Inc., P.O. Box 719, Uhrichsville, Ohio 44683, www.barbourbooks.com

Our mission is to publish and distribute inspirational products offering exceptional value and biblical encouragement to the masses.

 Member of the
Evangelical Christian
Publishers Association

Printed in China.